Table Of Contents

Introduction

Definition of UI Bakery

Definition of UI Bakery

UI Bakery is a no-code platform for creating web applications that offers a wide range of features to simplify the development process. It is the ultimate tool for beginners and intermediate no-code developers who are looking for a robust and user-friendly platform to design and develop their web applications.

UI Bakery includes a drag-and-drop interface that enables users to create web applications without having to write any code. It offers an extensive library of pre-built components, templates, and themes that allow developers to create visually appealing and responsive web applications in a fraction of the time it would take to build from scratch.

One of the key features of UI Bakery is its ability to integrate with other tools and services, such as third-party APIs, databases, and authentication services. This makes it easy for developers to add functionality to their web applications without having to write any code.

UI Bakery is also highly customizable, allowing developers to create their own custom components and templates. This means that developers can create unique and personalized web applications that meet their specific requirements.

UI Bakery offers a range of pricing plans to suit different budgets and needs. Its free plan offers limited features and is ideal for developers who are just starting out. Its paid plans offer more advanced features and functionality, making it ideal for professional developers who need more robust tools.

In conclusion, UI Bakery is a powerful no-code platform that offers an intuitive drag-and-drop interface and a wide range of pre-built components and templates. It is highly customizable and can be easily integrated with other tools and services, making it ideal for beginners and intermediate no-code developers who are looking for a robust and user-friendly platform to design and develop their web applications.

Benefits of using UI Bakery

As a beginner or intermediate NO Code developer, you may be wondering what tools and platforms are available to help you create stunning user interfaces for your applications. One of the most powerful and user-friendly options on the market today is UI Bakery.

UI Bakery is a drag-and-drop UI design tool that allows you to create beautiful and functional user interfaces without writing a single line of code. With UI Bakery, you can quickly and easily create responsive web apps, mobile apps, and desktop apps that look great and work seamlessly.

So, what are the benefits of using UI Bakery? Let's take a closer look.

1. No coding required

One of the biggest benefits of using UI Bakery is that you don't need to know how to code to use it. This means that even if you're a complete beginner with no experience in programming, you can still create stunning user interfaces that look and feel professional.

2. Easy to use

UI Bakery is designed to be intuitive and easy to use. The drag-and-drop interface makes it easy to add components and design elements to your user interfaces, and the platform provides a range of templates and pre-built components to help you get started.

3. Saves time

With UI Bakery, you can create high-quality user interfaces in a fraction of the time it would take to do it manually. This means you can focus on other aspects of your application development, such as coding and testing, and still deliver a polished and professional user experience.

4. Customizable

While UI Bakery provides a range of pre-built components and templates, you're not limited to these options. You can customize every aspect of your user interface to match your brand and meet the specific needs of your users.

5. Collaborative

UI Bakery is designed to be collaborative, which means you can work with your team members to create stunning user interfaces together. You can share your work in progress, get feedback, and make changes in real-time, making the design process faster and more efficient.

In conclusion, UI Bakery is a powerful and user-friendly tool that can help you create stunning user interfaces for your applications. With its intuitive drag-and-drop interface, customizable components, and collaborative features, it's a great choice for beginners and intermediate NO Code developers looking to take their user interface design skills to the next level.

Target audience

Target Audience

UI Bakery is a powerful no-code UI design tool that is designed to help beginners and intermediate no-code developers create stunning user interfaces without any coding experience. The tool is built for anyone who wants to design beautiful interfaces quickly and easily, without having to spend months learning how to code.

The target audience for UI Bakery includes individuals who are interested in building web and mobile applications, software engineers, designers, and entrepreneurs. The tool is ideal for those who are looking to create websites, blogs, e-commerce stores, and other online applications.

Beginners and Intermediate No-Code Developers

The tool is designed specifically for beginners and intermediate no-code developers who are looking for a simple and easy-to-use interface design tool. With UI Bakery, you can create stunning UI designs without any coding experience, making it an ideal choice for those who are just starting out in the no-code world.

UI Bakery Niches

UI Bakery is perfect for those who are looking to create dynamic and engaging user interfaces. The tool is ideal for creating responsive web designs, mobile applications, and other online applications that require a well-designed UI. UI Bakery can be used to create a variety of niches including:

1. E-Commerce Stores: With UI Bakery, you can create stunning e-commerce stores that are easy to navigate and visually appealing.

2. Web Apps: UI Bakery is perfect for creating web applications, allowing you to design interfaces that are both functional and visually appealing.

3. Mobile Apps: UI Bakery is designed to help you create mobile applications that are optimized for various screen sizes and devices.

4. Landing Pages: UI Bakery can be used to create landing pages that are designed to convert visitors into customers.

In conclusion, UI Bakery is an ideal no-code UI design tool for beginners and intermediate no-code developers who are looking to create stunning user interfaces without any coding experience. The tool is perfect for a variety of niches, including e-commerce stores, web apps, mobile apps, and landing pages. With UI Bakery, you can create beautiful and responsive interfaces quickly and easily, making it an invaluable tool for anyone looking to create a successful online presence.

Overview of the book

UI Bakery: The Ultimate NO Code UI Design Tool is a comprehensive guide to empower beginners and intermediate NO Code developers to create professional-grade web applications without writing a single line of code. This book is specially designed to explore the powerful features of the UI Bakery platform, a perfect blend of design and development tools that enable users to create stunning user interfaces that are both intuitive and appealing.

This book starts by introducing the concept of NO Code development, emphasizing its importance and benefits in the modern world of software development. It explains how NO Code platforms like UI Bakery have revolutionized the way developers build web applications, making it easier and faster to create visually appealing and functional interfaces without the need for coding expertise.

The book then delves into the core features of UI Bakery, highlighting its user-friendly interface, drag-and-drop functionality, and intuitive design tools. It provides step-by-step instructions on how to use the platform to create custom web applications, from simple landing pages to complex multi-page applications. Readers will learn how to create reusable components, define data models, and use the platform's built-in widgets to create dynamic and responsive interfaces.

In addition to the core features, the book also covers advanced topics such as integrating external APIs, customizing styles, and deploying applications to production. It provides tips and tricks to optimize the performance of applications and make them more accessible to users.

Throughout the book, readers will find practical examples, real-world scenarios, and use cases to help them understand the concepts and apply them to their own projects. The book is written in a clear and concise language, making it easy to follow and understand, even for readers with no prior experience in NO Code development.

Overall, UI Bakery: The Ultimate NO Code UI Design Tool is a must-have resource for anyone looking to enhance their skills in NO Code development and create stunning web applications quickly and easily.

Getting started with UI Bakery

Setting up UI Bakery

Setting up UI Bakery

UI Bakery is a powerful no code UI design tool that allows you to build complex and beautiful user interfaces quickly and easily. Whether you are a beginner or an intermediate no code developer, UI Bakery is an excellent choice for creating web and mobile applications without the need for coding.

To get started with UI Bakery, you need to set up your account. This process is straightforward and only takes a few minutes. Here is a step-by-step guide to help you set up your UI Bakery account:

Step 1: Visit the UI Bakery website

The first step is to visit the UI Bakery website. Here, you will find all the information you need to get started, including tutorials, FAQs, and pricing information.

Step 2: Sign up for an account

Once you are on the UI Bakery website, click on the "Sign up" button to create your account. You will need to provide your email address and create a password to access your account.

Step 3: Choose your plan

UI Bakery offers several pricing plans, including a free plan, a basic plan, and a pro plan. Choose the plan that best suits your needs and budget.

Step 4: Verify your email address

After you have chosen your plan, UI Bakery will send you a verification email to the email address you provided. Click on the link in the email to verify your account.

Step 5: Log in to your account

Once you have verified your account, you can log in to your UI Bakery account and start designing your user interface.

UI Bakery is a powerful no code UI design tool that is perfect for beginners and intermediate no code developers. With UI Bakery, you can create complex and beautiful user interfaces quickly and easily. Follow these simple steps to set up your UI Bakery account and start designing your user interface today.

Navigating the UI Bakery interface

Navigating the UI Bakery Interface

UI Bakery is a powerful no-code UI design tool that allows users to create stunning interfaces without the need for coding. However, like any tool, it can take time to master. In this chapter, we'll take a look at how to navigate the UI Bakery interface, so you can make the most of its features and create beautiful designs.

The Dashboard

When you first log into UI Bakery, you'll be taken to the dashboard. This is where you can access all your projects and templates. You can also create a new project from scratch or choose from a variety of templates to get started quickly.

The Editor

Once you've created a new project, you'll be taken to the editor. Here, you'll find all the tools you need to create your design. The editor is divided into two main sections: the canvas and the components panel.

The Canvas

The canvas is where you'll design your interface. It's a blank space where you can drag and drop components, arrange them, and style them to your liking. You can also adjust the size of the canvas to fit your needs.

The Components Panel

The components panel is where you'll find all the components you need to create your design. You can browse through a wide range of components such as buttons, forms, tables, and more. You can also customize these components to fit your design by adjusting their properties.

The Toolbar

The toolbar is located at the top of the editor and contains all the tools you need to create your design. You can access functions such as undo/redo, preview, and save from here. You can also access settings and account information from the toolbar.

Conclusion

In this chapter, we've covered the basics of navigating the UI Bakery interface. By familiarizing yourself with the dashboard, editor, canvas, components panel, and toolbar, you'll be able to create stunning designs in no time. With UI Bakery, you can create beautiful interfaces without the need for coding, making it the perfect tool for beginners and intermediate no-code developers.

Creating a new project

Creating a new project is the first step in designing an application or website using UI Bakery. It's an exciting moment, but it can also be intimidating, especially for beginners. However, with UI Bakery, you don't need to be a coding expert to create a polished and professional-looking project. Here's how to get started.

Step 1: Sign up and log in

Before you can start your project, you need to sign up for UI Bakery. Go to the website and create an account. Once you have an account, log in and select "New Project" from the dashboard.

Step 2: Choose a template

UI Bakery offers a wide range of templates to choose from, so you don't have to start from scratch. Browse the available templates and select the one that best fits your needs. You can always customize it later.

Step 3: Customize your template

Once you've chosen a template, you can start customizing it to fit your specific requirements. UI Bakery's drag-and-drop interface makes it easy to add and remove elements, change colors, and adjust layouts. You can also add your own images, icons, and text.

Step 4: Add functionality

UI Bakery offers a number of pre-built components that you can use to add functionality to your project. These include buttons, forms, and data tables. Simply drag and drop the component you want onto your design and customize it to fit your needs. You can also connect your project to external services like databases and APIs.

Step 5: Preview and publish

Once you've finished designing your project, you can preview it to see how it will look on different devices. UI Bakery offers a range of preview options, including desktop, tablet, and mobile. If you're happy with your design, you can publish it to the web with one click.

Creating a new project in UI Bakery is easy and intuitive, even for beginners. With its powerful features and intuitive interface, UI Bakery is the ultimate no-code UI design tool for anyone who wants to create stunning applications and websites without having to write a single line of code.

Understanding UI Bakery components

UI Bakery is a powerful no-code UI design tool that allows you to create stunning user interfaces for your web and mobile applications. In this subchapter, we will discuss the various components of UI Bakery and how they work together to create a seamless design experience.

First and foremost, UI Bakery is built around the concept of components. A component is simply a reusable building block that can be used to create a variety of different UI elements. For example, you might have a component for a button, a component for a form input field or a component for a menu.

These components are designed to be flexible and customizable, allowing you to easily modify their appearance and behavior to suit your specific needs. This means that you can create complex designs with ease, without having to worry about the underlying code.

One of the key advantages of using UI Bakery is that it provides a drag-and-drop interface that allows you to easily add, remove or modify components as needed. This makes it incredibly easy to experiment with different design ideas and iterate quickly until you find the perfect solution.

Another important component of UI Bakery is the layout system. This allows you to easily arrange and position your components on the page, ensuring that your design is both visually appealing and functional. The layout system is designed to be flexible and intuitive, allowing you to easily adjust the size, position and spacing of your components as needed.

Finally, UI Bakery also includes a range of other features and tools that can help you create beautiful and functional designs. These include built-in icons and images, custom styling options, and a variety of pre-built templates and themes that you can use as a starting point for your design.

Overall, UI Bakery is an incredibly powerful no-code UI design tool that provides a robust set of features and components that can help you create stunning designs with ease. Whether you are a beginner or an intermediate no-code developer, UI Bakery is a tool that should definitely be on your radar.

Designing with UI Bakery

Introduction to UI design

Introduction to UI Design

User interface (UI) design is the process of creating interfaces for software applications or digital devices that are user-friendly, visually appealing, and easy to navigate. UI design is a crucial aspect of software development, as it impacts the user experience and ultimately the success of the product. In this chapter, we will introduce you to the basics of UI design and how you can use UI Bakery, the ultimate no-code UI design tool, to create stunning interfaces for your projects.

The Importance of UI Design

UI design plays a critical role in creating a positive user experience. A well-designed interface can make it easy for users to navigate through an application or website, find the information they need, and accomplish their goals. On the other hand, a poorly designed interface can lead to frustration, confusion, and ultimately, a negative user experience.

UI design also has a significant impact on the success of a product. A visually appealing and user-friendly interface can help to attract and retain users, improve engagement, and increase conversions. In contrast, a poorly designed interface can lead to high bounce rates, low engagement, and low conversion rates.

UI Design Principles

To create a successful UI design, it is essential to follow certain principles. These principles include:

1. Consistency: Consistency in design helps users to understand how to use an application or website. It involves using the same design elements, such as fonts, colors, and icons, throughout the interface.

2. Simplicity: A simple interface is easy to navigate and understand. It involves minimizing the number of design elements and focusing on the most critical features.

3. Clarity: A clear interface is easy to understand and use. It involves using clear and concise language, as well as intuitive design elements.

4. Feedback: Providing feedback to users is essential for a positive user experience. It involves letting users know what is happening when they interact with an interface, such as when a button is clicked or when an action is completed.

Using UI Bakery

UI Bakery is the ultimate no-code UI design tool that allows beginners and intermediate no-code developers to create stunning interfaces for their projects. With UI Bakery, you can easily drag and drop design elements, customize the look and feel of your interface, and preview your design in real-time.

Whether you are designing a website, mobile application, or desktop software, UI Bakery makes it easy to create a user-friendly and visually appealing interface. With its intuitive design interface and powerful features, UI Bakery is the perfect tool for anyone who wants to create beautiful UI designs without any coding experience.

Conclusion

UI design is a crucial aspect of software development, and it is essential to follow certain principles to create a successful interface. UI Bakery is the ultimate no-code UI design tool that allows beginners and intermediate no-code developers to create stunning interfaces for their projects. With UI Bakery, you can easily create a user-friendly and visually appealing interface that will attract and retain users, improve engagement, and increase conversions.

Planning a UI design project

Planning a UI Design Project

UI design projects involve creating interactive and user-friendly interfaces that are easy to navigate and visually appealing. Whether you are a beginner or an intermediate NO code developer, planning is critical to the success of your UI design project. Below are some essential tips that you should consider before starting your UI design project.

Define the Goal of Your Project

Before you start designing, it is essential to have a clear understanding of the purpose of your project. You need to define the problem you want to solve, the target audience, and the expected outcomes. This will help you to create a design that meets the needs of your users and aligns with your business goals.

Conduct User Research

User research is critical to understanding your target audience's needs and preferences. It involves gathering data through surveys, interviews, and observation to help you design a user-friendly interface. This research will also help you to identify the pain points and challenges faced by your users, which can then address in your UI design.

Create a Wireframe

A wireframe is a basic skeletal structure that outlines the layout of your interface. It is a simple representation of your design that helps you to visualize the basic components of your user interface. This will allow you to test out different design ideas and make adjustments before moving on to the final design.

Choose the Right Tools

Choosing the right tools is crucial to the success of your UI design project. UI Bakery is the ultimate NO code UI design tool that allows you to create user-friendly interfaces without any coding knowledge. With UI Bakery, you can create visually appealing and responsive designs that are consistent across all devices.

Test and Iterate

Testing and iterating are critical components of the design process. It involves testing your design with real users and getting feedback on what works and what doesn't. This feedback will help you to refine your design and make improvements until you achieve the desired outcome.

In conclusion, planning is essential to the success of your UI design project. By defining your project's goals, conducting user research, creating a wireframe, choosing the right tools, and testing and iterating, you can create user-friendly interfaces that meet the needs of your users and align with your business goals.

Using UI Bakery components to design UI

Using UI Bakery components to design UI

UI Bakery is the ultimate NO code UI design tool that enables beginners and intermediate NO code developers to create stunning and functional user interfaces with ease. The platform provides a wide range of intuitive and customizable components that make designing UIs a breeze.

UI components are the building blocks of any UI design, and UI Bakery has a vast collection of them. From buttons, forms, and input fields to tables, charts, and graphs, UI Bakery components are designed to help you create a visually appealing and user-friendly UI that meets your needs.

One of the most significant advantages of using UI Bakery components is that you don't need to have any design or coding experience. The platform provides a simple drag-and-drop interface that allows you to add and customize components on your UI canvas with ease. You can choose from pre-designed templates or start from scratch and create your UI design from scratch.

UI Bakery components are also highly customizable, allowing you to adjust the size, color, and style of each component to match your brand identity or design preferences. You can also add animations, hover effects, and other interactive features to your components to enhance the user experience.

Another advantage of using UI Bakery components is that they are responsive, meaning they automatically adjust to different screen sizes, ensuring your UI looks great on any device. This feature comes in handy, especially for mobile app developers, who need to create UIs that work seamlessly on different screen sizes.

In conclusion, UI Bakery components are an excellent tool for beginners and intermediate NO code developers looking to create stunning and functional UIs without any coding or design experience. With a wide range of customizable components and a simple drag-and-drop interface, you can quickly create UIs that meet your needs and enhance the user experience.

Customizing UI design with UI Bakery

Customizing UI Design with UI Bakery

UI Bakery is a powerful no-code tool that allows beginners and intermediate no-code developers to create beautiful and functional user interfaces for their web or mobile applications. One of the key features of UI Bakery is its ability to customize the UI design to fit the specific needs of your project.

With UI Bakery, you have the ability to customize every aspect of your UI design, including the layout, colors, fonts, graphics, and more. This allows you to create a unique and personalized user interface that reflects your brand and your project's goals.

Layout Customization

One of the most important aspects of UI design is the layout. With UI Bakery, you have the ability to customize the layout of your user interface to fit the specific needs of your project. This includes the placement of buttons, menus, forms, and other UI elements. You can easily drag and drop UI elements onto your canvas and arrange them in any way you like.

Color Customization

Another important aspect of UI design is color. With UI Bakery, you have access to a wide range of color palettes and can easily customize the color of your UI elements to match your brand's color scheme. You can also create your own custom color palettes and save them for future use.

Font Customization

The font you choose for your user interface can have a big impact on how users perceive your application. With UI Bakery, you have access to a wide range of fonts and can easily customize the font size and style of your UI elements. This allows you to create a unique and personalized user interface that reflects your brand.

Graphics Customization

Finally, UI Bakery allows you to customize the graphics and images used in your user interface. You can easily upload your own images or use the built-in graphics library to find the perfect graphics for your project. You can also customize the size and placement of your graphics to fit your layout.

In conclusion, UI Bakery is an excellent tool for beginners and intermediate no-code developers who want to create beautiful and functional user interfaces for their web or mobile applications. With its powerful customization features, you can create a unique and personalized user interface that reflects your brand and your project's goals.

Styling with UI Bakery

Understanding UI styling

Understanding UI Styling

The look and feel of your user interface is critical to the overall user experience, and UI styling refers to the process of designing and customizing the visual elements of your application's interface. In this subchapter, we will explore the principles and best practices of UI styling that will help you create visually appealing and user-friendly interfaces.

UI Design Principles

Before we delve into the specifics of UI styling, it is essential to understand the fundamental principles of UI design. These principles will guide you in creating interfaces that are intuitive, engaging, and easy to use. Some of the key principles of UI design include:

1. Consistency: Consistency is crucial in creating a sense of familiarity and comfort for users. Consistent patterns, colors, and typography across the interface will help users navigate and use the application with ease.

2. Simplicity: The interface should be simple and easy to understand, with a minimalist design that avoids clutter and confusion. Users should be able to complete their tasks without distractions.

3. Visual Hierarchy: Visual hierarchy refers to the arrangement of elements on the interface based on their importance. The most important elements should be given more prominence, while less important elements should be less visible.

4. Accessibility: Accessibility is essential in ensuring that all users, regardless of their capabilities, can use the application. The interface should be designed with accessibility in mind, such as using high contrast colors and clear typography.

UI Styling Best Practices

UI styling involves customizing the visual elements of the interface to align with the principles of UI design. Some of the best practices for UI styling include:

1. Choosing the Right Colors: Colors play a vital role in UI design as they can evoke certain emotions and convey meaning. It is essential to choose colors that align with the brand, are visually appealing, and provide sufficient contrast for readability.

2. Typography: Typography is another critical element of UI design that can impact the overall user experience. The chosen fonts should be legible and easy to read, with an appropriate size and spacing.

3. Consistency: Consistency in UI styling is just as important as consistency in UI design. The use of consistent patterns, colors, and typography across the interface will help users navigate the application with ease.

4. White Space: White space refers to the empty space around the elements on the interface. The appropriate use of white space can help create a clean and uncluttered design, making it easier for users to focus on the content.

Conclusion

UI styling is an essential aspect of UI design that can impact the overall user experience. By following the principles and best practices of UI styling, you can create visually appealing and user-friendly interfaces that align with your brand and meet the needs of your users. With UI Bakery, you can easily customize your interfaces and create stunning designs without any coding skills.

Types of styles in UI design

When it comes to designing user interfaces, one of the most important considerations is the style. The style of a UI can greatly impact the overall user experience, and can make or break the success of an application. In this chapter, we will explore the different types of styles in UI design and what they entail.

Flat Design

Flat design is a popular style in UI design that has gained popularity in recent years. This style is characterized by a minimalistic approach that focuses on simplicity and clarity. Flat design features simple and bold shapes, bright colors, and a lack of gradients or shadows. This style is often used in mobile apps, websites, and other digital products.

Material Design

Material design is a design language developed by Google that is based on the principles of flat design. This style is characterized by the use of shadows and depth to create a sense of hierarchy and dimensionality. Material design also incorporates bold colors and typography to create a visually engaging UI. This style is often used in Android apps and other Google products.

Skeuomorphic Design

Skeuomorphic design is a style that mimics real-world objects and materials. This style is characterized by the use of textures, shadows, and other visual elements that create a sense of realism. Skeuomorphic design was popular in the early days of UI design, but has since fallen out of favor due to its tendency to be overly complex and difficult to navigate.

Minimalistic Design

Minimalistic design is a style that focuses on simplicity and functionality. This style is characterized by the use of white space, simple typography, and a lack of unnecessary visual elements. Minimalistic design is often used in web and mobile applications, and is particularly popular in the tech industry.

In conclusion, the style of a UI is a crucial aspect of design that can greatly impact the overall user experience. By understanding the different types of styles in UI design, you can create a UI that is both visually appealing and functional. Whether you choose a flat design, material design, skeuomorphic design, or minimalistic design, it is important to keep the user at the forefront of your design decisions. With the right style and approach, you can create a UI that is both beautiful and effective.

Applying styles to UI design with UI Bakery

Applying styles to UI design with UI Bakery

UI design is a crucial aspect of any application development process. It determines how users interact with your app and how they perceive your brand. Applying the right styles to your UI design can make a significant difference in how your app is received by your users. In this chapter, we will discuss how you can apply styles to your UI design using UI Bakery, the ultimate no-code UI design tool.

UI Bakery provides a wide range of styling options that you can apply to your UI design. From fonts to colors to padding and margins, UI Bakery has all the necessary styling tools to create a visually appealing UI design. The best part about UI Bakery is that you don't need to have any coding experience to apply these styles. All you need to do is drag and drop the styling options to your UI elements.

Fonts

Fonts are an essential aspect of UI design. They can help you convey a message, set a tone, and create a brand identity. UI Bakery provides a wide range of fonts that you can use to style your UI design. You can choose from various font styles, sizes, and colors to create a unique look for your app. UI Bakery also allows you to import custom fonts, giving you even more flexibility to create a unique look.

Colors

Colors play a crucial role in UI design. They can evoke emotions, convey information, and create a brand identity. UI Bakery provides a wide range of color options that you can use to style your UI design. You can choose from pre-defined color palettes or create your own custom color palette. UI Bakery also allows you to apply gradients and shadows, giving you even more flexibility to create a visually appealing UI design.

Padding and Margins

Padding and margins are essential for creating a clean and organized UI design. They help to create space between UI elements and improve the overall readability of your app. UI Bakery provides a simple drag and drop interface to apply padding and margins to your UI elements. You can easily adjust the spacing between UI elements and create a well-organized UI design.

Conclusion

UI Bakery makes it easy for beginners and intermediate no-code developers to apply styles to their UI design. With a wide range of styling options and a simple drag and drop interface, you can create a visually appealing UI design without any coding experience. Whether you're designing a simple landing page or a complex web application, UI Bakery has all the necessary styling tools to create a great UI design.

Advanced styling with UI Bakery

Advanced styling with UI Bakery

Once you have mastered the basics of UI design with UI Bakery, it's time to take your skills to the next level with advanced styling techniques. In this subchapter, we'll explore some of the more advanced features of UI Bakery that can help you create stunning and unique user interfaces.

1. Custom CSS

UI Bakery comes with a built-in CSS editor that allows you to customize the look and feel of your application. With custom CSS, you can change the font, color, size and position of any element in your design. You can also add animations and effects to make your app more engaging.

2. Advanced Grid Layouts

Grid layouts are a powerful tool for creating responsive designs that look great on any device. UI Bakery has a drag-and-drop grid layout editor that lets you create complex layouts quickly and easily. You can also customize the spacing between elements and adjust the size and position of each grid cell.

3. Dynamic Styling

UI Bakery allows you to create dynamic styles that change based on user interactions. For example, you can change the color of a button when the user hovers over it, or animate an element when it's clicked. This can help make your app feel more interactive and engaging.

4. Custom Themes

If you want to create a unique look and feel for your application, UI Bakery allows you to create custom themes. You can choose from a variety of pre-built themes or create your own from scratch. This gives you complete control over the style of your application and helps set it apart from other apps.

5. Integration with Design Tools

UI Bakery integrates with popular design tools like Sketch and Figma. This allows you to import your designs directly into UI Bakery and continue working on them from there. This can help streamline your workflow and save you time.

In conclusion, UI Bakery is a powerful tool that allows beginners and intermediate NO code developers to create stunning and unique user interfaces. By exploring the advanced styling techniques outlined in this subchapter, you can take your skills to the next level and create truly remarkable applications.

Adding Interactivity with UI Bakery

Introduction to interactivity

Introduction to Interactivity

Interactivity is the ability of a user interface to respond to user inputs or actions. It allows users to engage with the interface, perform tasks, and accomplish goals. Without interactivity, a user interface would be static and unresponsive, making it difficult for users to interact with it.

Interactivity is an essential aspect of user experience design. A good user experience is one that is intuitive, efficient, and satisfying. Interactivity plays a crucial role in achieving these goals. It helps users to navigate through the interface, perform tasks, and accomplish their goals easily and efficiently.

The importance of interactivity cannot be overstated. It is what makes a user interface engaging and easy to use. It is what sets apart a good user interface from a bad one. Interactivity can be achieved through various means, such as buttons, menus, sliders, forms, animations, and feedback.

Buttons are one of the most common forms of interactivity. They allow users to perform actions such as saving, deleting, or submitting data. Menus are another common form of interactivity. They allow users to navigate through the interface and access different features and functionalities.

Sliders are a form of interactivity that allows users to adjust values, such as the volume or brightness. Forms are another form of interactivity that allows users to input data and perform tasks such as logging in or registering.

Animations and feedback are also essential forms of interactivity. Animations can provide visual cues to users, such as indicating progress or completion of a task. Feedback can provide users with information on the success or failure of their actions.

UI Bakery is a no-code UI design tool that allows beginners and intermediate no-code developers to create interactive user interfaces easily and efficiently. It provides a range of features and functionalities that enable users to create buttons, menus, sliders, forms, animations, and feedback.

In conclusion, interactivity is an essential aspect of user experience design. It allows users to engage with the interface, perform tasks, and accomplish goals. UI Bakery provides a range of features and functionalities that enable users to create interactive user interfaces easily and efficiently. With UI Bakery, beginners and intermediate no-code developers can create engaging and user-friendly interfaces that provide a great user experience.

Adding basic interactivity with UI Bakery

Adding basic interactivity with UI Bakery

Are you tired of creating static designs that don't engage your users? Do you want to add basic interactivity to your UI designs without writing a single line of code? Look no further than UI Bakery, the ultimate no-code UI design tool!

With UI Bakery, you can easily add basic interactivity to your designs using simple drag-and-drop actions. Whether you want to create clickable buttons, interactive menus, or dynamic forms, UI Bakery has got you covered.

To get started, simply select the element you want to add interactivity to and click on the "Actions" tab in the properties panel. From here, you can choose from a variety of pre-built actions, such as "Go to page," "Open modal," "Submit form," and more.

For example, let's say you want to create a clickable button that takes the user to a different page. Simply select the button element and click on the "Actions" tab. Then, select the "Go to page" action and choose the page you want to link to. That's it! Now, when the user clicks on the button, they will be taken to the specified page.

You can also add basic interactivity to forms by using UI Bakery's built-in form elements. For example, you can add a "Submit" button to a form and use the "Submit form" action to send the form data to your backend. You can also use the "Show message" action to display a success or error message to the user after they submit the form.

In addition to pre-built actions, UI Bakery also allows you to create custom actions using JavaScript. This is a great option for more advanced no-code developers who want to add more complex interactivity to their designs.

With UI Bakery, adding basic interactivity to your UI designs has never been easier. Give it a try today and take your designs to the next level!

Adding complex interactivity with UI Bakery

Adding complex interactivity with UI Bakery

UI Bakery is a powerful no-code UI design tool that enables users to create stunning interfaces quickly and easily. It offers a wide range of features and functionalities that enable designers to add complex interactivity to their designs without any coding skills.

In this subchapter, we will explore how to add complex interactivity to your UI designs using UI Bakery. We will cover the following topics:

1. Understanding the basics of interactivity

Before we dive into the nitty-gritty of adding interactivity to your UI designs, it is essential to understand the basics of interactivity. In simple terms, interactivity refers to the ability of a user to interact with an interface. This can be achieved through various elements such as buttons, sliders, and input fields.

2. Using widgets to add interactivity

UI Bakery offers a wide range of widgets that can be used to add interactivity to your designs. These widgets include buttons, checkboxes, sliders, and input fields. You can easily drag and drop these widgets onto your canvas and customize them to suit your needs.

3. Creating dynamic components

UI Bakery also allows you to create dynamic components that can respond to user actions. For instance, you can create a dropdown menu that displays different options based on the user's selection. You can achieve this by using UI Bakery's conditional visibility feature.

4. Working with events

Events are triggers that occur when a user interacts with a UI element. UI Bakery allows you to add event handlers to your widgets, which can be used to trigger a specific action when a user interacts with the element. For example, you can add an event handler to a button that displays a message when clicked.

5. Using data binding

Data binding is a powerful feature that allows you to bind UI elements to data sources. This enables you to create dynamic interfaces that can display real-time data. UI Bakery offers a simple and intuitive data binding feature that allows you to bind UI elements to data sources in just a few clicks.

In conclusion, UI Bakery is a powerful no-code UI design tool that enables designers to add complex interactivity to their designs without any coding skills. By using widgets, dynamic components, events, and data binding, you can create stunning interfaces that are highly interactive and engaging. Whether you are a beginner or an intermediate no-code developer, UI Bakery is the ultimate tool for creating stunning UI designs.

Testing interactivity with UI Bakery

Testing Interactivity with UI Bakery

As a NO Code developer, one of the most important aspects of creating a user interface is testing for interactivity. This involves ensuring that all the elements on the interface are responsive and functional, and that the user flow is smooth and intuitive. Fortunately, UI Bakery makes testing interactivity easy and seamless.

UI Bakery comes with a built-in testing feature that allows developers to preview their interfaces and test for interactivity before publishing them. This feature is especially useful for beginners and intermediate NO Code developers who are still learning how to create user interfaces and want to ensure that their interfaces are functional and user-friendly.

To test interactivity with UI Bakery, simply click on the preview button in the top right corner of the screen. This will open a preview window that displays the interface in its entirety. From here, you can interact with the interface just as a user would, clicking on buttons, filling out forms, and navigating through the different pages.

As you interact with the interface, UI Bakery will automatically update the preview window, allowing you to see how the interface looks and functions in real-time. This makes it easy to identify any issues or bugs in the interface, and make adjustments as needed.

In addition to the built-in testing feature, UI Bakery also supports integrations with external testing tools, such as Testim and Cypress. These tools allow developers to automate the testing process and run tests on multiple devices and browsers, ensuring that the interface is functional and responsive across all platforms.

Overall, testing interactivity with UI Bakery is a straightforward and intuitive process that can help developers create user interfaces that are both functional and user-friendly. Whether you are a beginner or an intermediate NO Code developer, UI Bakery provides all the tools you need to create high-quality interfaces that meet the needs of your users.

Integrating UI Bakery with other tools

Integrating UI Bakery with no-code development tools

Integrating UI Bakery with no-code development tools

UI Bakery is a powerful no-code UI design tool that allows you to create stunning user interfaces without writing a single line of code. However, UI design is just one part of the development process. To create a fully functional web or mobile application, you need to integrate your UI with backend services and other functionality. This is where no-code development tools come in.

No-code development tools are designed to help you build complete applications without having to write any code. They provide a visual interface for creating and configuring different parts of your application, making it easy for beginners and intermediate developers to build complex applications without any coding skills.

Integrating UI Bakery with no-code development tools can help you create powerful and complex applications quickly and easily. Here are some of the benefits of using UI Bakery with no-code development tools:

1. Faster development: By integrating UI Bakery with no-code development tools, you can create complete applications in a fraction of the time it would take to write all the code yourself.

2. Easier collaboration: No-code development tools make it easy to collaborate with other developers and stakeholders. By using a visual interface, everyone can see what's happening in the application and provide feedback.

3. More flexibility: No-code development tools provide a lot of flexibility in terms of what you can build. You can create custom workflows, integrate with different APIs, and more.

4. Lower costs: By using UI Bakery with no-code development tools, you can reduce the cost of development. No-code development tools are often more affordable than hiring developers, and you can create applications in-house without having to outsource.

Some popular no-code development tools that can be integrated with UI Bakery include Bubble, Appy Pie, and Adalo. Each tool has its own strengths and weaknesses, so it's important to do your research and choose the one that best fits your needs.

In conclusion, integrating UI Bakery with no-code development tools is a great way to create powerful applications quickly and easily. By using a visual interface, you can create complex workflows, integrate with different APIs, and collaborate with other developers and stakeholders. Whether you're a beginner or an intermediate no-code developer, integrating UI Bakery with no-code development tools can help you take your applications to the next level.

Integrating UI Bakery with coding tools

Integrating UI Bakery with Coding Tools

UI Bakery is an excellent no-code UI design tool that empowers beginners and intermediate no-code developers to create stunning web applications without any coding knowledge. However, for those who would like to enhance their applications further, integrating UI Bakery with coding tools can be a game-changer.

Integrating UI Bakery with coding tools like React, Angular, and Vue.js can help no-code developers achieve more customization, flexibility, and functionality in their web applications. Additionally, it can also speed up the development process by enabling no-code developers to reuse code snippets and components.

One of the primary benefits of integrating UI Bakery with coding tools is the ability to use custom code snippets in UI Bakery's drag-and-drop interface. No-code developers can create custom code snippets in their preferred coding tool and import them into UI Bakery, saving them time and effort.

Another benefit of integrating UI Bakery with coding tools is the ability to use pre-built UI components. Coding tools like React, Angular, and Vue.js offer a wide range of pre-built UI components that can be integrated into UI Bakery to create more complex applications.

Integrating UI Bakery with coding tools also enables no-code developers to use APIs and third-party libraries to add more functionality to their web applications. APIs and third-party libraries can be integrated into UI Bakery using custom code snippets, providing no-code developers with even more flexibility and customization options.

In conclusion, integrating UI Bakery with coding tools can help beginners and intermediate no-code developers take their web application development to the next level. It offers more customization, flexibility, and functionality options, as well as speeding up the development process. By integrating UI Bakery with coding tools like React, Angular, and Vue.js, no-code developers can create stunning web applications that are both beautiful and functional.

Integrating UI Bakery with other design tools

Integrating UI Bakery with other design tools

UI Bakery is a powerful no-code platform that is designed to help developers create stunning user interfaces without writing a single line of code. But, what if you want to use it in conjunction with other design tools? Fortunately, UI Bakery is designed to integrate seamlessly with other popular design tools, allowing you to create beautiful designs quickly and easily.

One of the most popular design tools that UI Bakery integrates with is Sketch. Sketch is a powerful vector graphics editor that is widely used by designers around the world. With UI Bakery, you can easily import your Sketch designs into the platform and use them to create interactive user interfaces. This is a great way to save time and ensure that your designs are consistent across all platforms.

Another popular design tool that you can integrate with UI Bakery is Figma. Figma is a cloud-based design tool that is designed to help teams collaborate on designs. With UI Bakery, you can easily import your Figma designs into the platform and use them to create stunning user interfaces. This is a great way to ensure that your designs are consistent across all platforms and that your team is working together effectively.

In addition to Sketch and Figma, UI Bakery also integrates with other popular design tools like Adobe XD and InVision. No matter what design tool you prefer to use, UI Bakery makes it easy to integrate your designs into the platform and create beautiful user interfaces quickly and easily.

Integrating UI Bakery with other design tools is a great way to save time and ensure that your designs are consistent across all platforms. Whether you prefer to use Sketch, Figma, Adobe XD, or InVision, UI Bakery makes it easy to integrate your designs and create stunning user interfaces. So, if you're a beginner or intermediate no-code developer, be sure to explore the possibilities of integrating UI Bakery with your favorite design tools.

Troubleshooting integration issues

As a NO Code developer, one of the most important skills you need to have is the ability to troubleshoot integration issues. Integration is the process of connecting different software applications to work together seamlessly. However, sometimes, the integration process may not go as planned, and you may run into issues that require troubleshooting.

Here are some common integration issues that you may encounter and some tips on how to troubleshoot them:

1. Authentication issues: Authentication is the process of verifying the identity of a user or application. If you are having issues with authentication, check that you have entered the correct username and password. Also, make sure that the authentication settings are correctly configured in both applications.

2. Data mapping issues: Data mapping is the process of converting data from one format to another. If you are having issues with data mapping, check that the data mappings are correct and that the data is being mapped to the correct fields.

3. Connection issues: Sometimes, you may have issues with the connection between the two applications. Check that the connection settings are correct and that the network connections are functioning correctly.

4. Permissions issues: Permissions determine what actions a user or application can perform. If you are having issues with permissions, check that the permissions are correctly set up in both applications.

To troubleshoot integration issues, you should first identify the problem. Once you have identified the problem, you can then try to isolate the issue by testing each component of the integration separately. For example, if you are having issues with authentication, you can try logging in to each application separately to see if there are any issues with the authentication process.

In addition, it is important to document the steps you have taken to troubleshoot the issue. This will help you to keep track of what you have tried and what has worked and what has not.

In conclusion, troubleshooting integration issues is an essential skill for NO Code developers. By following the tips in this chapter, you can identify and troubleshoot integration issues quickly and effectively, ensuring that your applications work seamlessly together.

Best practices for using UI Bakery

Creating accessible UI designs with UI Bakery

Creating accessible UI designs with UI Bakery

Designing accessible user interfaces is crucial for any product, ensuring that all users can access and use the application with ease. In this subchapter, we will take a look at how UI Bakery can help beginners and intermediate NO Code developers create accessible UI designs.

One of the key features of UI Bakery is its ability to offer accessible components and design elements that can be used to build accessible user interfaces. These components include buttons, text fields, dropdowns, and more, which can be customized to meet the needs of users with disabilities.

UI Bakery also offers accessibility guidelines that developers can follow to ensure that their design meets the standards of the Web Content Accessibility Guidelines (WCAG) 2.1. These guidelines provide a clear understanding of what needs to be implemented to ensure that the interface is accessible to all users.

Another feature that makes UI Bakery a great tool for designing accessible user interfaces is its ability to create responsive designs. This means that the interface can be adapted to different screen sizes and resolutions, making it accessible to users on different devices.

With UI Bakery, developers can also test the accessibility of their designs using the built-in accessibility checker. This checker provides feedback on any accessibility issues that may exist within the interface, helping developers to make the necessary changes to improve accessibility.

In conclusion, UI Bakery is an excellent tool for beginners and intermediate NO Code developers looking to create accessible user interfaces. Its accessibility components, guidelines, responsive design features, and accessibility checker make it easy to design interfaces that are accessible to all users, regardless of their abilities. By following the accessibility guidelines provided by UI Bakery, developers can ensure that their interface is accessible to everyone, making their product more inclusive and user-friendly.

Optimizing UI designs for performance

Optimizing UI designs for performance is crucial for creating a great user experience. As a beginner or intermediate NO Code developer using UI Bakery, you have the power to create stunning UI designs with ease. However, it is essential to optimize your designs to ensure that they load quickly and smoothly.

One of the key factors that affect UI performance is the size of the assets used in your design. Large images and videos can slow down the loading time of your page, causing frustration for your users. To optimize your designs for performance, it is best to use compressed images and videos that are optimized for web use. This will reduce the file size of your assets without compromising the quality of your design.

Another important factor is the use of animations and transitions in your design. While animations can enhance the user experience, excessive use of animations can slow down the performance of your page. When using animations, it is best to keep them simple and use them sparingly. Additionally, you can use CSS animations instead of JavaScript to reduce the load time of your page.

Optimizing the layout and structure of your page can also improve the performance of your design. Use a grid layout to ensure that your page is neatly organized, and use white space to give your design a clean and uncluttered look. This will not only improve the performance of your page but also enhance the readability of your content.

Finally, it is crucial to test your designs on different devices and browsers to ensure that they load quickly and smoothly. Use tools like Google PageSpeed Insights and GTmetrix to analyze the performance of your page and make necessary optimizations.

In conclusion, optimizing UI designs for performance is vital for creating a great user experience. By using UI Bakery, you have the power to create stunning designs without any coding skills. However, it is essential to optimize your designs by using compressed assets, simple animations, grid layouts, and testing on different devices and browsers. With these tips, you can ensure that your designs load quickly and smoothly, providing an excellent user experience for your audience.

Collaborating with others on UI design projects with UI Bakery

Collaborating with others on UI design projects with UI Bakery

UI design is essential for creating any digital product, and collaboration is key to designing a successful user interface. UI Bakery is a powerful no-code UI design tool that enables you to create beautiful, functional user interfaces without writing any code. However, you may need to collaborate with other designers, developers, or stakeholders to create the best UI for your project. Fortunately, UI Bakery makes collaboration easy.

In this subchapter, we will explore how you can collaborate with others on UI design projects using UI Bakery. We will cover the following topics:

1. Sharing your project with others

One of the most important steps in collaborating with others on UI design projects is sharing your project with them. UI Bakery allows you to share your project with others by providing a shareable link. You can simply send this link to your collaborators, and they can access your project from their browser.

2. Collaborating in real-time

UI Bakery provides real-time collaboration tools that allow you to work with your collaborators simultaneously. You can see their changes as they make them, and they can see your changes as you make them. This feature enables you to work together on the same project, regardless of your location.

3. Commenting and feedback

UI Bakery allows you to add comments and feedback to your project. You can use this feature to communicate with your collaborators, provide feedback on their work, and suggest changes. This feature makes it easy to keep track of your project's progress and ensure that everyone is on the same page.

4. Version control

UI Bakery provides version control tools that allow you to keep track of your project's progress. You can create multiple versions of your project, and you can revert to an earlier version if necessary. This feature makes it easy to collaborate with others without worrying about losing your work.

In conclusion, UI Bakery is an excellent tool for collaborating with others on UI design projects. Whether you are working with other designers, developers, or stakeholders, UI Bakery provides the features you need to create an effective user interface. By using the real-time collaboration tools, commenting and feedback, and version control features, you can work together to create the best UI for your project.

Staying up-to-date with UI Bakery updates and features

Staying up-to-date with UI Bakery updates and features is crucial for beginners and intermediate NO code developers who want to stay ahead in the game of designing user interfaces without writing a single line of code. UI Bakery is constantly upgrading its features and tools to make the UI design process easier, faster, and more efficient.

One way to stay up-to-date with UI Bakery updates and features is to subscribe to their newsletter. The UI Bakery newsletter is an excellent way to get the latest updates on new features, improvements, and bug fixes. Additionally, the newsletter also includes useful tips, tutorials, and best practices to help you make the most out of UI Bakery. The newsletter is free, and you can sign up on the UI Bakery website.

Another way to stay up-to-date with UI Bakery updates and features is to follow them on social media. UI Bakery maintains an active presence on platforms like Twitter, LinkedIn, and Facebook. Following them on social media will keep you informed about the latest updates, upcoming features, and other important news. Additionally, you can also interact with other users, ask for help, and share your experiences using UI Bakery.

UI Bakery also provides documentation for its features and tools. Reading the documentation is an excellent way to learn about the features and tools in detail. The documentation includes step-by-step tutorials, use cases, and examples that will help you understand how to use UI Bakery effectively. You can access the documentation on the UI Bakery website.

Finally, UI Bakery also offers support to its users. If you have any questions or encounter any issues while using UI Bakery, you can contact their support team. The support team is available round the clock and can help you resolve any issues you may face. You can contact them through email or the chat feature available on the UI Bakery website.

In conclusion, staying up-to-date with UI Bakery updates and features is essential for beginners and intermediate NO code developers who want to design user interfaces quickly and efficiently. By subscribing to the newsletter, following them on social media, reading the documentation, and seeking support when needed, you can make the most out of UI Bakery and stay ahead of the curve.

Conclusion

Summary of the book

UI Bakery: The Ultimate NO Code UI Design Tool is a comprehensive guide that provides a detailed overview of UI design tools and techniques that can be used by beginners and intermediate NO code developers. The book is written to help individuals who are looking to design and develop user interfaces without the need for coding skills.

The book begins by introducing the concept of NO code development and its benefits over traditional coding. It then goes on to explain the various tools and techniques used in UI design, including wireframing, prototyping, and user testing. The author provides a step-by-step guide to each of these tools and demonstrates their practical application in the UI design process.

One of the key features of UI Bakery is its intuitive drag-and-drop interface, which allows users to create stunning user interfaces with ease. The book provides a comprehensive overview of how to use this tool, including its features, settings, and customization options. The author also shares tips and tricks on how to optimize the tool to achieve the best results.

In addition to the practical aspects of UI design, the book also covers the theoretical concepts that underpin effective user interface design. The author explains the principles of usability, accessibility, and user experience, and provides examples of how these principles can be applied in UI design.

Overall, UI Bakery: The Ultimate NO Code UI Design Tool is an essential guide for anyone looking to develop user interfaces without the need for coding skills. It provides a comprehensive overview of the tools and techniques used in UI design, as well as practical tips and tricks for creating stunning interfaces. Whether you are a beginner or an intermediate NO code developer, this book is an invaluable resource that will help you take your UI design skills to the next level.

Benefits of using UI Bakery

UI Bakery is a no-code UI design tool that offers a wide range of benefits for both beginners and intermediate no-code developers. The tool is designed to help you create beautiful and functional user interfaces without the need for coding.

One of the biggest benefits of using UI Bakery is the time savings. With the tool's drag-and-drop interface, you can quickly create UI design prototypes in a matter of minutes. This means that you can spend more time on other aspects of your project, such as testing and refining your designs.

Another benefit of using UI Bakery is the ease of use. The tool is designed to be user-friendly, with intuitive controls that make it easy to navigate and create designs. Whether you're a beginner or an experienced no-code developer, you'll find the tool easy to use and understand.

UI Bakery also offers a high degree of customization. You can choose from a variety of pre-built components and templates, or you can create your own custom components from scratch. This gives you complete control over the look and feel of your designs, and allows you to create unique and personalized user interfaces.

The tool also offers collaboration features, which allow you to work with other members of your team in real-time. This means that you can share your designs and get feedback from other team members, which can help you to refine your designs and make them even better.

Finally, UI Bakery offers excellent support and documentation. If you ever have any questions or issues with the tool, you can easily reach out to the support team for help. Additionally, the tool comes with extensive documentation and tutorials, which can help you to learn how to use the tool quickly and efficiently.

In conclusion, UI Bakery is an excellent no-code UI design tool that offers a wide range of benefits for both beginners and intermediate no-code developers. With its time-saving features, ease of use, customization options, collaboration features, and excellent support and documentation, it's the perfect tool for anyone looking to create beautiful and functional user interfaces without the need for coding.

Future of UI design with UI Bakery

The future of UI design with UI Bakery is exciting and full of possibilities. With the rise of no-code development tools, designers and developers can create stunning interfaces without writing a single line of code. UI Bakery is one of the best no-code UI design tools that has made it possible for beginners and intermediate no-code developers to create professional-grade interfaces with ease.

UI Bakery is a drag-and-drop interface builder that allows users to create beautiful and functional interfaces by simply dragging and dropping elements onto the canvas. It comes with a wide range of pre-built components, templates, and widgets that users can customize to suit their needs. With UI Bakery, designing interfaces has become an enjoyable and creative process that requires no coding skills.

The future of UI design with UI Bakery is all about making the process of designing interfaces faster, easier, and more intuitive. UI Bakery is constantly evolving and improving to meet the needs of its users. With new features and updates being added regularly, UI Bakery is set to become the go-to tool for no-code designers and developers.

One of the exciting things about the future of UI design with UI Bakery is the possibility of integrating it with other no-code tools. This integration will make it possible for designers and developers to create complete applications without writing a single line of code. The future of UI design with UI Bakery is all about making the process of designing and building interfaces faster, easier, and more efficient.

In conclusion, the future of UI design with UI Bakery is bright and full of possibilities. As the demand for no-code development tools continues to grow, UI Bakery will continue to evolve and improve to meet the needs of its users. With its intuitive interface, pre-built components, and constant updates, UI Bakery is the perfect tool for beginners and intermediate no-code developers looking to create stunning interfaces with ease.

Resources for further learning about UI Bakery.

Resources for Further Learning about UI Bakery

UI Bakery is a powerful no-code tool that allows beginners and intermediate no-code developers to create stunning user interfaces and web applications with ease. If you're interested in learning more about UI Bakery and taking your skills to the next level, there are a number of resources available to help you along the way.

Here are some of the top resources for further learning about UI Bakery:

1. UI Bakery Documentation - The UI Bakery documentation is an excellent resource for beginners and intermediate no-code developers who are just getting started with the tool. It provides detailed information about the UI Bakery interface, as well as step-by-step instructions for creating various types of user interfaces and web applications.

2. UI Bakery YouTube Channel - The UI Bakery YouTube channel is a great resource for visual learners who prefer to watch tutorials and walkthroughs. The channel features a variety of videos that cover everything from getting started with UI Bakery to more advanced topics like working with data and integrating with other tools.

3. UI Bakery Blog - The UI Bakery blog is a valuable resource for anyone interested in staying up-to-date with the latest news and trends in the no-code space. It features articles on a wide range of topics, including UI design, app development, and no-code tools and platforms.

4. UI Bakery Community - The UI Bakery community is a great place to connect with other no-code developers and get help and support with your projects. It's a friendly and welcoming community where you can ask questions, share your work, and learn from others.

5. UI Bakery Academy - UI Bakery Academy is an online learning platform that offers courses and tutorials on UI design, app development, and no-code tools and platforms. It's a great resource for anyone looking to take their skills to the next level and learn from industry experts.

In conclusion, UI Bakery is a powerful no-code tool that offers a wealth of resources for beginners and intermediate no-code developers. Whether you prefer to learn through documentation, videos, blog posts, community forums, or online courses, there are plenty of resources available to help you master this powerful tool and create stunning user interfaces and web applications.

www.ingramcontent.com/pod-product-compliance
Lightning Source LLC
LaVergne TN
LVHW051742050326
832903LV00029B/2671